SERIOUSLY

BONKERS

[SB]

Silver Bullet's Scrap book

by

Herb Miller

ISBN 978-0957548343

A catalogue record for this book is available from the British Library

Published by: Susan Cowe Books

Printed by: CreateSpace

Scene Building

In the early nineties, Herb Miller led a product development project code named Silver Bullet. The team started collecting pairs of words where the first started with an S and the second with a B.

We called them SB's and recorded them in the SB list.

The **seriouslybonkers.com** website (also known as **bigram.co.uk**) is the continuation of that part of the project.

This short book, being published to celebrate the author's special birthday, is a derivative of the website.

Every SB in this book should appear in the website.

But not vice-versa.

Supportive Blurb

What people have said about this project

Simply Brilliant, Bill Jinks

Seriously Bonkers, Greg Penoyre

Silly Bunt, Trevor Bishop

What people have said before

Stupid Boy, Capt. Mainwaring

What people might have said

Socrates Bettered, Plato

Story, Blah, Nigel Tomm

So Bitty, David Walliams

What should be said

Super, Brilliant

So British

Sensationally Brave

Supplied By

I'd like to thank the following people for their help in gathering the SBs, some being reproduced here.

Silver Bullet & other IBM projects

Jon Woodcock, Gill Woodcock, Chris Cross, Simon Murton, Gordon Hutchison, Sarah Booth, Greg Loten, Chris Winter, Bill Jinks, Bill Kelly, Hilma Miles, Mike Glennon, Dave Morgan, Suren Johanssen, Tim Carpenter (SSE 2006), Andy (Biggles) Anderson, Peter Green, William Portal, Peter Drury, Jon Isaac, Ajay Gita Radhakrishnan, Mike Ford.

Rowlands Castle Golf Club

Andy Wood, Mark Wilcox, John Boyd Brown, Keith Broomfield, Trevor Bishop, Doug Murgatroyd, and other long suffering bit hunters at the Wednesday gentleman's roll up.

Madrid, Scotland and Hampshire

Susan Cowe Miller, Jim Clark, Irene Clark, Jim Hunter, Jean Wilson.

Family and friends

Trevor, Sue and Steph Brown, Graeme and Louise Cowe, Kate Miller, Greg Penoyre, Chrissie Teitge, Malcolm Bowden, Denise Thatcher, Ray and Marjorie Thomas, Peter and Beth Miller, Rachel Cowe, Tony and Christine Price, Ava Mae Cowe, Greg and Sian Browne, Sarah (Maysie) Mayes, Mike Ridge, Alex Lewis, Dave Lewis, Gary and Zoe Grant, Louise Lynton-Evans, Katy Taylor, Barbara Herd.

Herb Miller

WordPressers

John & Simon Blackbourn, Graham Armfield, Mike Pead, Sim Brody, Jonny Allbut, Spameur Bonaldi, Tim Nash, Andrew Leonard, Jenny Wong, JJ Jay, Dan Westhall.

Others

Frederick P Brooks Jr., Michael Parkinson, Stephen Fry, Richard Curtis, Josh Widdicombe, Stanley Baxter, Eric Idle, Jane Cooke, David Millar.

Self Bio

Herb Miller lives in Rowlands Castle with his wife and two cats.

He's been collecting SBs for nearly half his lifetime.

If you ask him why he'll say 'Simply because'.

His favourites to date are the short but sweet, palindromic Sub bus, the Sulphurous Brewmasters Googlewhack and of course, Seriously Bonkers, Simply Brilliant and Silly B.

He fully expects his short booklet to become a shortlisted bestseller.

Starting blocks

Selected Bits

Semi-biographical

Small	Boy	Jul 1965
Silver	Bullet	1990-1991
Sulphurous	Brewmasters	Aug 2005
Sete	Bordeaux	Jul 2008
Swinging	Boat	Jan 2011
Stansted	Beeches	May 2011
Sandy	Bit	May 2011
Shiny	Bucket	Feb 2015
Selle	Bassano	Jun 2015
Sergeant	Bramble	Oct 2015
Spanish	Break	Apr 2016
Shade	Bathing	May 2016
Startled	Birds	Aug 2016
Still	Bobbing	Oct 2016
Slur	Building	Nov 2016
Still	Breezy	Nov 2016
Squeeze	Ball	Nov 2016
Scenic	Brittany	Dec 2016
Stubborn	Blighter	Mar 2017
Super	Breakfast	Apr 2018

Small Boy
Jul 1965

I was a small boy when I was younger. Sister's bigger. This photo was probably taken on my seventh birthday at Marloes beach, a long sandy beach in St. Brides Bay. We had plywood surf boards which we used like body boards. The sand brushed against my nipples giving me sore boobs.

Silver Bullet
Oct 1990-1991

Well this is where the search for SBs started, in 1990. Silver Bullet was the name of a project I worked on in IBM. My boss, Chris Winter, came up with the name after Fred Brook's book 'The Mythical Man Month'. In this book Fred states that there is no such thing as the Silver Bullet. My job was to try to construct some software that re-used existing best of breed components in an attempt to disprove Fred. Obviously we failed.

But we had great fun trying.

It wasn't until 2010 that I learnt that a pair of words are known as a bi-gram. If you have more words then they become n-grams. Isn't Wikipedia marvellous?

Anyway, if you do a Google search for Silver Bullet nowadays you will find a host of different uses.

- To kill werewolves
- A type of Scooter
- A rapper
- A vibrator
- A drink from Coors
- Book by Stephen King
- A law enforcement supply company
- Music venue in Finsbury park
- Not forgetting Bob Seger's Silver Bullet Band

Sulphurous Brewmasters

18 Aug 2005

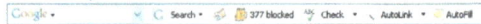

After returning from a holiday in France, and having listened to a CD of Dave Gorman's Googlewhack Adventures, I started my own search for a Googlewhack. Naturally I limited myself to searching for an SB Googlewhack. I eventually found it and recorded it for posterity.

The original link is still available:
http://hbd.org/hbd/archive/933.html

Sete Bordeaux

30 Jul 2008

10 years ago I cycled along the tow path of the Canal du Midi from Bordeaux to Sete, with my friend Trevor and my partner Susan driving the support bus.

I wonder what I was thinking as I was rounding the lighthouse in the Bassin-du-Thau. Was I contemplating the return journey, from Sete to Bordeaux?

More likely stay balanced, you don't want to fall into that salty brine on your special birthday.

Swinging Boat
Jan 2011

At Emsworth I took a series of photos of a small boat swinging in the breeze with the sun bursting through the clouds over Hayling. I combined 7 different views into one image and used it to create an advertisement in the Coast and Downs directory. *Swing into action with your integrated website and blog.* In Aug 2016 I re-used the image in my snazzy banner for the shortcode based plugin called oik-bob-bing-wide.

Stansted Beeches

2 May 2011

Which do you prefer the least,

facing West or facing East?

Not facing East nor facing West;

neither picture's second best.

15

Sandy Bit

29 May 2011

A Sandy bit is an award that you receive in the following situation.

- You are playing golf at Rowlands Castle Golf Club
- It's the men's Wednesday evening roll up
- Your ball has entered a greenside bunker "in regulation"
- You get down in two strokes
- Therefore you have a gross par... Which is known as a Sandy Par

So you win a BIT (25p).

Of course it's also possible to play better than par and get a

Sandy Birdie.

I've never done that.

Shiny Bucket

4 Feb 2015 – 6 Nov 2016

Whether this is a steel bucket or silver bucket doesn't bother this soft bear as much as it bothers me that I've had this as my screen background on my iPad for a very long time without realising its relevance.

I first used the photo when writing my bucket list for WordCamp Birmingham UK (7-8 Feb 2015).

Selle Bassano

18 Jun 2015

It took me over 20 years to notice what was printed on my saddle's backside. It's a handmade Italian saddle. No wonder it's so brilliant.

Sergeant Bramble
24 Oct 2015

Hello, my name is Bramble. I live in Redhill Road. 41's the number. That's something I've been told.

I'm not allowed out the front door, the cat flaps at the rear. So I visit neighbour's gardens, some far – but mostly near.

Well, that's what Herb and Susan think, that I live at their house. I'm happy to go anywhere, where dinner's not just mouse.

So if you see me visiting, please take a pic of me. And send it to those people who live next to 43.

19

Spanish Break

April 2016

Scottish belle

Skinny bee

Stolen belt

Susan's bag

Sparse bonnet

Stewarton banker

Sunny bit

Stone balls

Sixtieth birthday

Spit bunkers

Susan brace

Soya butter

Spanish bitch

Sienna bucket

Part of the collection of SB's from Jim's sixtieth birthday celebrations. This list includes several brilliant ones; spermy breeks, Segway brigade, stenographer's bestie, sawny bean and Sponish Barder.

Shade Bathing
17 May 2016 & 16 Jul 2017

Hello, my name is Marmalade. I live in Redhill Road. I like chasing birds and mice and once I caught a toad. In our garden there's a pond. It's full of little fishes. When I'm hungry, I im-ag-ine them served in food dishes. I share my home with Bramble of whom you must have read. And a couple of them human things who have a comfy bed. They don't mind me getting on it, when my paws are clean. But when I'm wet and dirty, the Scot's one - she gets mean! The other one sits in his room tap-tap tap-tapping away. But sometimes, when I visit him, he takes a break to play. I quite like finding places where I hide out of sight. I need lots of rest by day...
I'm out hunting all night.

Startled Birds

25 Aug 2016

Startled birds fly away. Settle back another day.

Still Bobbing

13 Oct 2016

13th October 2016 was bobbing wide's seventh birthday. I was asked by Jane Cooke if I was still bobbing. Answer: yes.

This photo was on my Facebook page for bobbingwideweb

Slur Building
7 Nov 2016

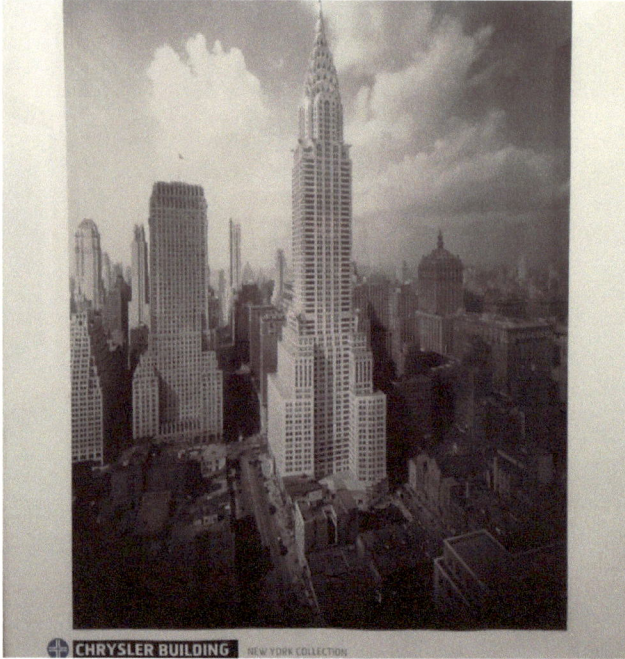

I believe it's safe to publish this now that the presidential election is over. Every time I see this poster, in our downstairs loo, I ignore the **Chry**, misread the *sler*, and smile broadly at the thought of slur building.

I wonder who started it. I imagine it was politicians travelling around the country on their slander buses.

PS. And now I've looked up *sler* in the urban dictionary and discovered that it's cool to say 'Don't you just love that sler building'.

Still Breezy
24 Nov 2016

When I got up on the 24th November 2016, I looked out of the window and noted that it was still breezy. It's not something you find on the Beaufort Scale. This photo, taken at Hayling in January, was edited from a still of a video, catching the waves as they crashed into the sea barrier protecting the stony beach.

So it was a strong breeze then, and it's still breezy now.

Squeeze Ball

25 Nov 2016

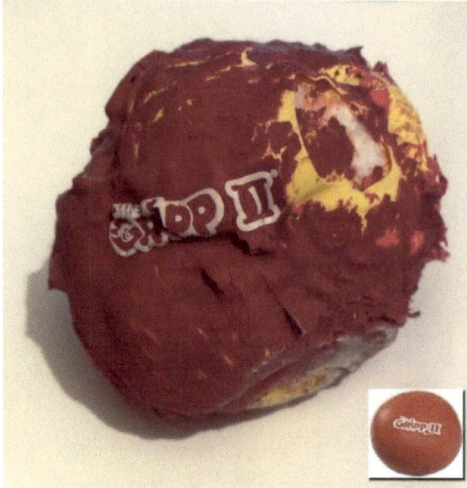

I noticed that my Gravatar profile read as follows...

Herb Miller is a WordPress specialist from Rowlands Castle, Hampshire, UK. In 2009 he travelled to the Far East with a Gripp II squeeze ball *and started writing a blog at* thegrippii.wordpress.com *– entitled "The gripping adventures of a* squeeze ball*". He now spends most of his time developing plugins for oik-plugins.*

Note: The photograph shows the ball in its current state, the insert shows the original. The Gripp II is no longer squeezable, but it does still help reduce stress. Thanks to Ajay Gita Radhakrishnan for giving it to me all those years ago.

Scenic Brittany
22 Dec 2016

The cote sauvage at Portivy. In the distance we watched a lone surfer.

I didn't see the surf breaking and ended up with soggy boots.

Herb Miller

Stubborn Blighter

21 Mar 2017

Until recently we had two gates to the road. Apart from days when the wind has blown them, they've never been shut. They were showing signs of aging. I decided it was time to take them down. This screw delayed the process somewhat. Having failed to loosen it with an impact screwdriver I tried drilling it out. That failed too, so I resorted to brute force with a crow bar. I'm pleased to report that one gate has now been removed and dismantled. Not sure what to do with all the ironmongery yet.

Super Breakfast
28 April 2018

Sausage, bacon, scrambled, beans and something brown, supplied by Hurtmore GC, set me up for my best round of golf ever. This photo may have been shot badly, but my golf wasn't. Lots of pars, but only a single birdie.

Herb Miller

Section B

A structured breakdown, separated by subject basis.

Some Background

The Silver Bullet project's list of words was originally written on paper and known as the SB list.

It was typed up into a plain text file called SB.txt. This file eventually contained 1425 entries. Each pair of words (known as an SB) was given a single letter classification. When they were imported into WordPress this was converted into a Category.

	Meaning	Example	To
-	OK	Silver Bullet	SB
b	brand name	Sensor Blade	Some Business
c	cheat	Sauteed Bunny	Silly Blogger or Skipping Bigrams
d	disastrous failure	Banana Splits	Seriously Bad
f	foreign	Sacre Bleu	Said By
n	name	Sergeant Bilko	Some Body
p	place	Sunset Boulevard	Site Base
q	questionable	Stripy B	Skipping Bigrams
s	sick or stupid	Safe Bonk	Silly Blogger
x	x-rated	Silly Bunt	Shocking Behaviour
i	Image	photo	Seen By
j	jpeg	screen capture	Surf Bite

The two image categories were not considered in the 90's. Other categories have subsequently been added as the site evolved.

Sorted By

Since so many of the original entries from the SB list were undated, in the automatic creation process I attributed 30th July 1991 to them – my birthday.

I have now found evidence of some being logged before that date.

The entry for the 6th May indicates I was typing up the list after a long weekend cycling around the Isle of Wight.

In the website, the entries are Sorted By the date they were created, newest first.

Sampled Bigrams are given the same date as the Source Bigram.

Said By

Words spoken by real people. Sound bites. Possibly
in a foreign language.

Salette Blanc Seems Believable Same Bracket Sorry
But Sacre Bleu Saltim Bocca Sand Berm Sauf
Bus Sea Boy Selbst bedienung Specialite Bretonne

Sampled Bigram

A sampled bigram is one that's created implicitly.

Several Bathing Sherfield Brewery Strictly
Boringly Sampled Brews Single Birdie Small
Breakfast Sale Bin Shown Boldly Starry Blobs Sign
Before Surely Beckons Some Balls Sink Below Soft
Bedding Small Bunnies Shadow Broker Sparrow
Bothering Stives Bakery Stuffed Baguettes Sells
Buns Seals Basking Sealless Beach Sell Beauty Skin
Base Shared Bathroom Sizeable Bladder Shitting
Bananas Sticks By Shan't Buy Synchemicals
Brushwood Safari Best Say But Some
Bookks Sodding Box Surprising Behaviour Small
Black Somehow Baulked Solar Bulbs Shine
Brightly Stratford But Shakespeare's Best Seldom
Bought Sunday Bargain Shakespeare's
Birthplace Seek Bright Spherical Balls Shaped
Base Scotlands Best Sugar Butter Scones
Bannocks Sampling Both Scottish Berry Soda
Based Some Beers Submit Bigram Slightly
Bothersome Sold By Small Breadsticks Supplemental
Book

Sandy Bits

Golf related

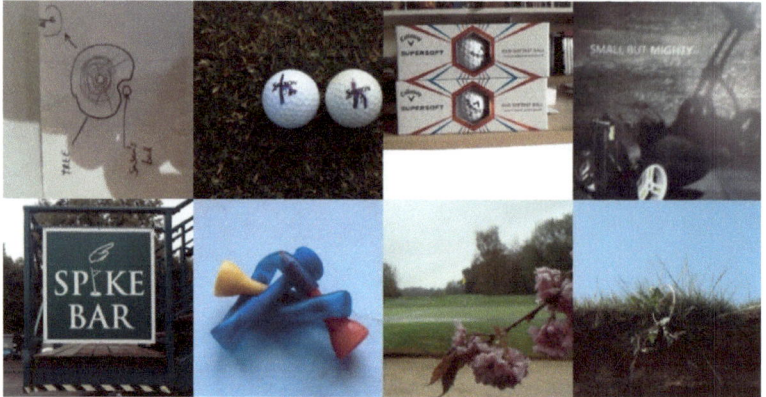

Stony Bunker Sprinkle Bugs Slippery Bank Susan's
Ball Spare Battery Starter's Bench Sandy Bottom
Stupid Ball Softtop Buggy Severiano
Ballesteros Sand Bunker So Bad Simpler Birdie Six
Blob Scoring Better Slightly Below Single
Birdie Some Balls Several Blobs Sinking Birdie Sandy
Birdie Shag Bag Stymied Ball

SB

The default classification for a bi-gram. Originally populated from the SB list for every single bigram. See Some Background.

Sheep Brooch Scallop Boat Solitaire
Board Schweppes Bubbles Scottish Blood Scottish
Barley Swing Bridge Smash Box Stress
Begin Susan's Ball Stranger Bug Strange Bug Sewer
Below Sesame Baguettini Sipper Bottles Stationary
Bike Stubborn Blighter Sg Big Seaside Bahrain

Scottish Blend

Scottish business.

Shaggy Beast Surely Bliss Skye Batiks Scottish
Baking Scotland's Beginning Stornoway Black
Scottish Blood Scottish Barley Scotch Broth Scottish
Birds Smokie Bible Scottish Buildings Singing Butler
Sea Birds Silver Bowl Scottish Breakfast Sky
Bond Scottish Blossom Scottish Breaded Scotch Beef
Signals Bistro

Seen Before?

Searched bigrams where the S-word and B-word have separately been used in other bigrams but not yet combined into their own searchable blob.

While writing the Seriously Bonkers book I worked on a local copy of the website. I found myself searching for many SBs that I didn't think I'd used before. Having written the code to create Sampled Bigrams, generated from existing content, I then looked what I could do for all the SBs that we've missed.

Given that there are already 1100 S-words and 950 B-words the site could contain over a million SB's. But who would think of combining Selfish with Brontosaurus, Sadistic with Bedwetter or Seen with Before?

… Some bugger would.

I decided to improve the Search Behaviour to not only say "Sorry, but" but also to create Seen Before entries when the S-word and B-word had both been seen before.

I'd fill in some blanks later.

Seen By

A photograph of something with SB.

Smart Basket Sustainably Brewed Sunflower
Bread Super Bright Solid Bordeaux Spell
Bound Sexual Behaviour Smart Brain Solid
Bloke Smart Brabus Source Book Storm
Brewing Shelly Beach Salisbury Bound Scotch
Beef Summer Bodies Sweet Brown Skirting
Board Saving Box Supported By Small
Boquets Shower Buddy Strikes Back Shuttle
Bus Sunday Brunch Something Borrowed

Seriously Bad

Originally classified as disastrous failure. These are entries which are NOT SB's. There shouldn't be many of these.

We should be using this category for invalid entries; signifying something's broken.

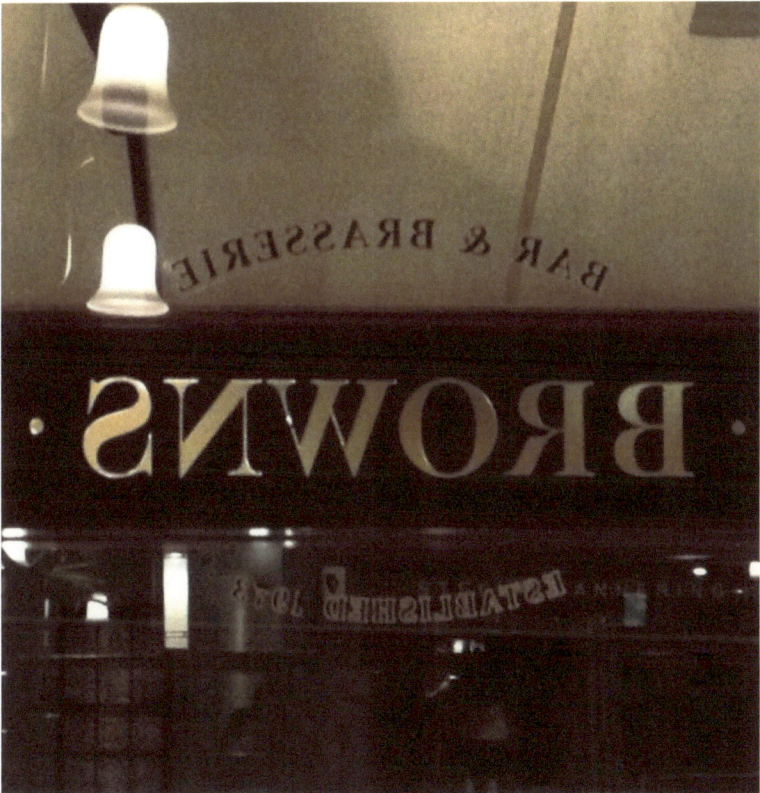

Smus Buddy Slatri Bizmuth Banana Splits Business FactorTable Sb Sb Supersticious Beliefs

Seriously Bonkers

Simply bonkers, surprisingly built, so barmy. The sort of bigrams I might have used when searching for an SB Googlewhack.

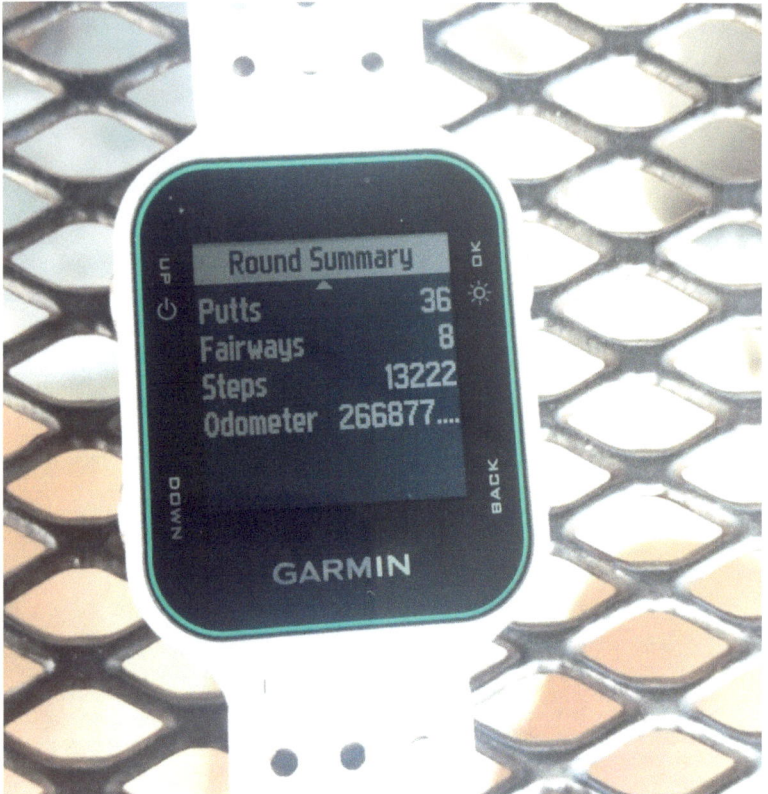

Sizeable Bounds Slug Balancer Shadow Borkers Smart Bbboing Small Blue Snot Butter Scale Bonkers Snub Buns Sub Bus Suffering Bit Selfish Brontosaurus Skinned Bat Skinned Budgie Snow Business

Shocking Behaviour

Represents X-rated or risque entries such as 'Secret Bonk'.

I had no idea what a sladge bunkle might be. I just used it as some test data. Then I found both sladge and bunkle in the Urban Dictionary.

I'll be more careful with my choice of words in the future.

Sarcastic Bugger Shag Bag Snotty Bastard Sweaty Bollocks Saturday Bonk Shit Bag Sodden Bangladeshi Sweaty Buttocks Saucy Bugger Shitty Bottom Sodding Bigwhitebox Swift Bonk Savage Bastard Shrewd Bastard Sodomised Bum Swinging Bollocks Scheming Bitch Sick Bangladeshi Sperm Bag Scouse Bastard Silly Buggers Spicy Bottom Screaming Bastards Silly Bunt Spilled Beans Scruffy Bugger Silver Bootleg Spotty Bum Secret Bonk Silver Bullshit Spunky Bottom Selfish Bastard Simon Bigmouth Spunky Bubble Sensational Bollocks Slimy Bastard Squeaky Bra Sadistic Bastard Sensational Boobs Slippery Bonk Squealing Bastards Sadistic Bedwetter Sensitive B...(its) Slow Bonk Starving Bangladeshi Sadistic Bigamist Serious Ballsup Smelly Bollocks Stretched Bowels SadoMasochistic Bondage Serious Bullshit Smelly Bum Stupid Bastard Sanctimonious Bastard Severe Bollocking Smug Bastard Sunday Bonk

Shot Badly

Photos or images that appear Somewhat Blurred or are Sized Badly i.e. not square boxes. There shouldn't be too many of these! We'll see.

Silly Blogger

A rather stupid entry or something found in a blog.

Shining Brasso Somebody's brainchild Subliminal
Badgering Sb Bi Stop Blogging Start Bigramming
Stub Buts Semi Billion Super Brilliant Splendid Batch
Season's Best Spangled Banner Stagnant
Boarhole Sheep Box Shredded Beet Silent
Burglar Silent Butler Silk Band Silver Bacofoil Skinny
Bop Spangled Banner Stagnant Boarhole Star Brake
Safe Bonk Starched Bloomers Sandstone
Block Sauteed Bunny

Single Byte

SB's where there's only one letter in the S or B word.
Sometimes both.

An S and a B in square brackets is used as the favicon for the website.

Site Base

A place or location. e.g. Santa Barbara, Sunset Boulevard

Skipping Bigrams

Represents cheats or questionable entries such as 'Sausage Beans' which should be 'Sausage and Beans' or 'Sausage, Beans'

So British

So very British!

Sixpenny Bit

Found while weeding the front hedge, this coin, which is 10 years older than me and therefore has a picture of George VI on the other side, has remained stubbornly brown even though I did attempt to clean it up with a soda bath. Soda being the generic term Americans use for fizzy drinks like Coca Cola. I tried diet coke (it wasn't fizzy), WD40 and Viakal. Perhaps I should have tried a scrubbing brush. I imagine some bright spark will suggest Brasso, Sodium Bicarbonate or strong brandy.

I quite like it the way it is.

Software Based

Terms associated with the software business.

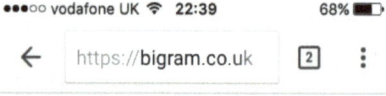

●●●○○ vodafone UK 📶 22:39   68% 🔋

←   https://bigram.co.uk   2   ⋮

🗎

This page isn't working

bigram.co.uk unexpectedly closed the connection.

ERR_CONTENT_LENGTH_MISMATCH

Strange Bug Supported Browsers Spam Blocker Sniffing Browser Site Building Seriously Broken Single Blog Scheduled Blog Summertime Bug Section Break Shortcode Based Sand Box S B Software Based Sorting By Serif Bold Seven Bit Sign Bit Sixteen Bit Sixtyfour Bit Size Border Skill Builder Slider Bar Smalltalk Bigot Software Backlog Software Bug Software Builders **Business FactorTable** Space Bar Selection Button Square Brackets Semantic Block Static Binding Sense Byte Square Brackets

Sold By

Brand or Company name.

Sultana Bran Super Bock Stain Block Stain
Block Special Bitter Sun Brite Saucy Bucketful Smelly
Balls Scorpio Blue School Bars Scooby-doo
Burger Sausage Bacon Sun Baby Strawberry
Brulee Spider Bite Sovereign Bitter Salad
Bowl Saison Beer Sleep Bright Signature
Burgers Strawberry Bear Samsonite Barbour Swing
Ball Sensory Ball Silver Bath Smart Builders Spinach
Beet Southern Belles Soul Bird Square Bubbles

Some Body

Someone's name.

If a particular name or photo happens to be yours and uniquely identifies you, but you don't want it to appear on the site, then let me know and I'll remove it. Conversely, if you think you should be listed then let me know.

Sean Beecher Simon Burrows Spandau Ballet Steve Bauer Sad Bloke Sarah Burdett Simpson Bart Spider Boy Steve Bikko Scott Bosworth Sinclair Bain Spoilt Bastard Steve Blame Sally Barker Scott Bright Sir Bennet Squirt Boat Stevie B Sally Bartram Sen Biden Sister Bernadette St. Bartholomew Stoney Bridge Sally Bowles Sergeant Bilko

Some Business

A company name, not necessarily a brand name.

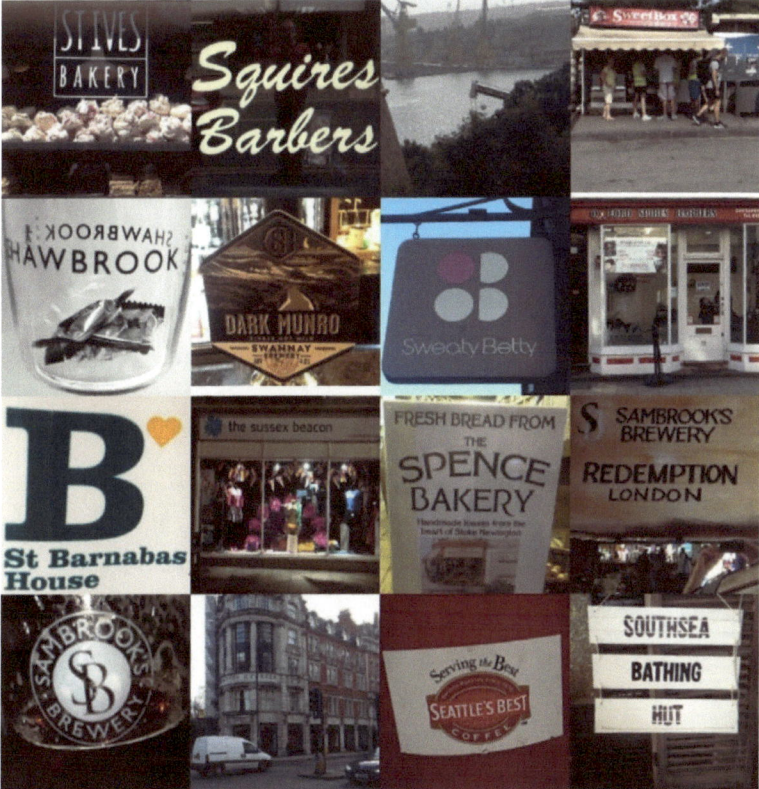

Shipyard Brewing Sanu Babu Surefix Building Soul
Bowl Selle Bassano Shaeffer Ballpen Squosh
Bottle Shimano Bearings Stabilo Boss Shimano
Brakes Stanley Blades Sigart Bulletin Star Bingo
Slazenger Bag Stolen Beginnings S- box Slazenger
Balls Strepsils Box

Someone's Book

Either the author's name, the title or something else that caught my eye while surreptitiously browsing. I have actually purchased and read some of them.

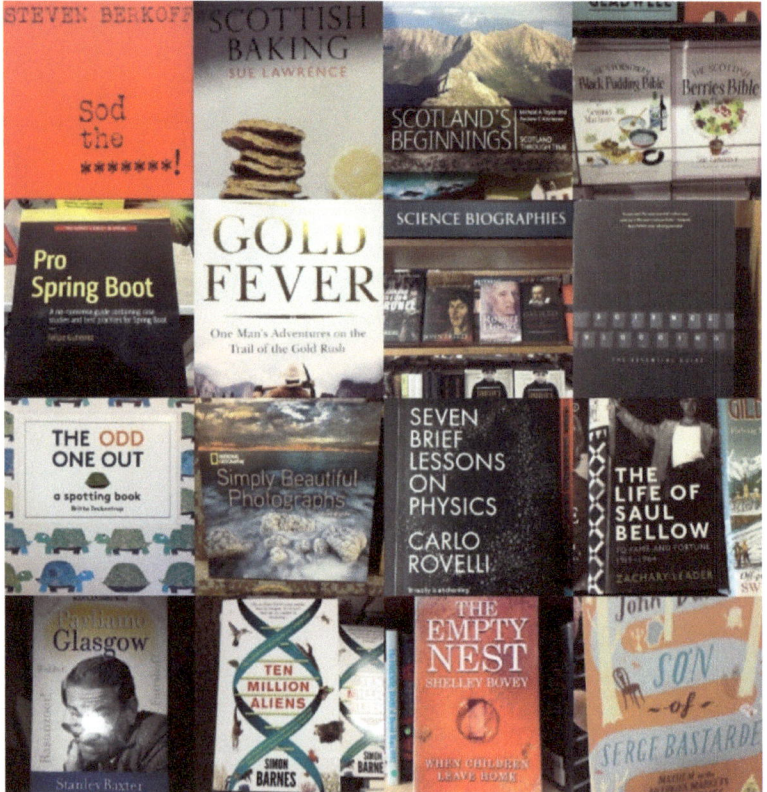

Surf Bite

A screenshot of an SB bigram used in the content.
Different from Seen by, but not that different.

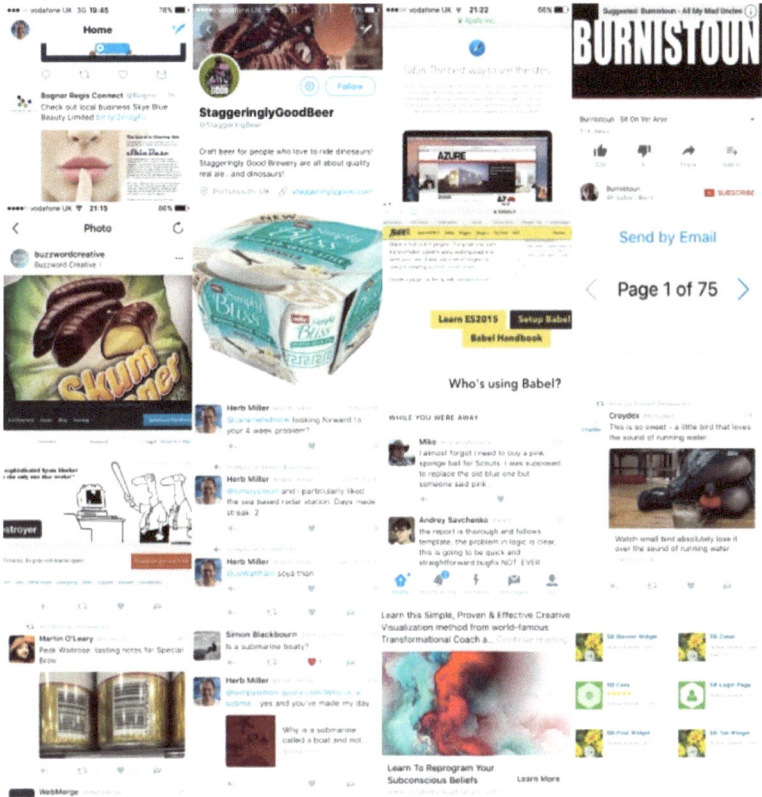

Specially Built

Structured Browsing

The seriouslybonkers.com and bigram.co.uk websites have a specially built theme designed to display SBs in various groupings.

The main menu is organised rather like the book.

The side bar provides some boxes to guide your browsing.

- Sequentially Biased
- Summed By
- Structured Breakdown
- Site Building

The footer contains the most popular S words and B words.

Click on the links to view the contents or list. You may find some beauties.

Search Box

Use the search box to see if we've already recorded your favourite SB.

The results page recognises that you may know many more SB's than the website does.

But you may not be the first person to come up with an SB. A Seen before count is displayed and incremented for each bigram that appears first on the page.

No one likes to see 'Sorry, but...' so I've written some code to automatically generate new entries in the Seen Before? category. The system doesn't always generate a new bigram. But it will do when the search consists of one S-word and one B-word, both terms have been used before and you're a logged in user.

Submit Bigram

If you would like to submit a bigram to the website then you'll need a login. You could consider asking me for an ID. But I won't give you one. I like to manage the entries myself.

It's not a wiki after all. The website is a diary of sorts; semi biographical in nature and supposedly random.

I use the Submit Bigram page to do all the hard work of publishing an SB picture, categorise it and to give it a few words.

So boo!

Share Bigrams

If you want to share a new SB then you can tweet to the @SharedBigram Twitter account.

You might also want to create your own SBs on a sharing board such as the SB list on Pinterest.

https://www.pinterest.co.uk/bobbingwide/sb-list/

Susan bullied me into adding that you might want to start building your own list on Instagram.

SEO Busting

The SB page, written in React JS, uses the WordPress REST API to operate as a Single Page Application.

It saves a bit of typing. Just click on the second letter of the S-word or B-word to see the list of bigrams that match. Here I chose BB.

Then choose one of the listed SBs. E.g. Smart Bbboing.

I've no idea what Google makes of this page!

Seriously Bonkers

The Silver Bullet project team
had a quirky twist,
collecting pairs of random words
into the *SB list*.

Mid '91 they had 1K,
then several hundred more,
but Herb said he could double it,
"of that you can be sure".

Now 2 years short of 30,
the list *has* got much longer,
with digital colour photographs
to make the content stronger.

A dedicated website
contains the latest list.
seriouslybonkers.com
a site not to be missed.

If you don't like to go online,
you might just want to look,
at selected bits of the *SB list*,
now published as a book.

The rules are very simple.
Find two words: **S** and **B**.
If you don't try to make one up,
you're not normal... like me!

www.ingramcontent.com/pod-product-compliance
Lightning Source LLC
Chambersburg PA
CBHW042124290326
41934CB00001BA/2